The Love of Three Oranges

The Love of Three Oranges

A play for the theatre that takes the commedia dell'arte of Carlo Gozzi
and updates it for the new millennium

By
Hillary DePiano

Based on the scenario *L'amore
Delle Tre Melarance* by Carlo
Gozzi, 1761

Original Cast

This version of *The Love of Three Oranges* was first performed February 22nd, 2002 in Tustin Studio Theatre at Bucknell University, Lewisburg, PA with the following cast:

Narrator. . . . . Matthew A. Griffin *either*

Silvio, King of Hearts. . . . . .Stephen J. Pinciotti *Guy*

Pantalone/Donkey. . . . . John Godfrey *either/or*

Prince Tartaglia. . . . . T. Patrick Halley *male*

Princess Clarice. . . . . Bekah Clark *female*

Leandro/Bumpkin 1. .J. C. Whittaker *male*

Truffaldino. . . . . Robert McGarvey *either*

Brighella. . . . . Mike Moran *male*

Smeraldina. . . . . Rachel Slotcavage *women*

Fata Morgana. . . . . Hollie Barattolo *women*

Farfarello/Palace Guard/Bumpkin 3/Cook. . . . . . Kyle McGee *either*

The Wind God/Mute Bumpkin/Rope. . . . . Jack Gendron *either*

Creonta. . . . . .Brittany Bohn *women*

A gate/Palace Guard/Bumpkin 2. . . . . .Josh Beckerman *either*

Princess Nicoletta/Nurse. . . . . .Emma V. Stefanski *women*

Princess Linetta/Servant. . . . . Liz Grasing *women*

Princess Ninetta. . . . . Ashi Day *women*

Musician. . . . . Colin Aherne *either*

Direction. . . . . Hillary DePiano

Stage Manager. . . . . Renee Awad

Assistant Stage Managers. . Lacy Gonzalez, Karen Johnson

Movement Coach. . . . . Mark Olsen

Costume Design. . . . . Paula Davis-Larson

Scenic Design. . . . . .Guerry Hood

Lighting Design. . . . . Heath Hansum

Special Thanks and Dedication

The creation of this play and subsequent performances were the result of work by tons of people to each of whom I owe more thanks than I will ever be able to give. Most especially, I have to thank the following Bucknell staff members for their tireless devotion and guidance over the course of this project: Jean Peterson, Paula Davis-Larson, Pam Miller and the costume shop (for making beautiful oranges under extreme pressure), Heath Hansum, Elaine Williams, Guerry Hood, Chris Fry, Gary Grant and, of course, the indescribable Bob Gainer.

In addition to those listed above, I have to also thank Matt, T. Pat, Rob, John, JC, Kyle, Josh, Mike, Bekah, Liz, Hollie, Ashi, Jack, Emma, Brittany, Rachel, Colin, KJ, Lacy and most especially Renee for their improvisational touches, hard work, sense of humor and for being as devoted to this play as myself. So much of this work is yours; I cannot thank you enough for your help.

And lastly neither the play, the production, nor the publishing would have occurred without the hard work and devotion of Steve Pinciotti. From running off copies, skipping class to paint the set, running extra rehearsals, doing tons of editing on his own time, keeping the director/playwright from breakdown and still managing to be a great King Silvio, I am forever indebted to him for all his help and support.

This play is dedicated to Carlo Gozzi. If he is rolling in his grave, let's hope it's with laughter.

Introduction

"Here ended the second act, which had been followed
with more marked applause than the first. My bold
experiment began to seem less culpable than it had
done at the commencement." -Carlo Gozzi

For centuries, commedia dell'arte reigned as one of the most popular forms of comedy. With stock characters, masks and set pieces of slapstick, the professionals who performed it entertained generation after generation and so many elements of it still define comedy to this day. But, in 1761, the classical form of the style had all but died out. While elsewhere the comedies of Moliere were the vogue, the favorite playwright of Italy was Carlo Goldoni. Though Goldoni's comedies drew from the commedia dell'arte, the characters were transformed into sympathetic characters and the stories relied upon drama and wordplay rather than physical comedy. The Italian theatre was ripe for a change.

Though theatre wars and playwright rivalries were very common and popular in Venice, perhaps the most famous one began when (according to literary legend) Goldoni encountered Count Carlo Gozzi, an outspoken essayist who had been lambasting Goldoni's plays for some time in articles and pamphlets, in a bookstore. The offended Goldoni challenged Gozzi, saying that if he objected so much to his plays, why didn't he write a better one?

Gozzi, a self proclaimed authority on comedy (in so much as he knew what did not work within Goldoni's works) also held the professionals of commedia in high regard and sought to revitalize that faltering genre. He saw his rival's challenge as the perfect opportunity to both achieve a triumph of pride and to reinvent the commedia form.

Confident in his ability, he selected a simple and well known children's story as the basis for his narrative. By using the simplest possible story and the mass appeal of the fairy tale form, Gozzi penned his first play, an embittered and scathing parody of Goldoni and his work entitled *The Love of Three Oranges*. Utilizing the floundering commedia dell'arte troupe of his friend Antonio Sacchi, he wrote only a simple scenario with a few set speeches (most to deliberately parody Martellian verse or the elevated prose of Goldoni's peer Voltaire that Gozzi also despised) and left most open to the talents of the actors. The show itself, with its sketchy outline of a plot, was little more than an extended caricature of Goldoni and Chiari (another rival playwright) and the style of their plays. Much of its humor was redundant and juvenile mockery, yet the play itself was a huge success.

The original scenario itself, written in paragraph form, is heavily peppered with commentary from Gozzi himself. While some is very clearly written as reflections upon the first performance of the play, most is detailed (and redundant) explanations of each of his choices as an author and why each joke is funny. He spells out how and where he is parodying his rivals in the text and notes with a good deal of glee that his audience did indeed recognize his jabs and greeted them with laughter.

Yet Gozzi's influence was twofold for, while he did succeed in turning over the stagnant comic trends in Venice in his time, he also breathed new life into commedia dell'arte, one that could survive in the modern era. He had bested his rivals in their own game and emerged on top both intellectually and monetarily as his plays achieved great financial success. But, more importantly, he had used his knowledge of comedy to revitalize a simple story into a highly successful comic work, shaking the very foundations of established theatre in his time and encouraging growth and change.

~

As a director working in this millennium, however, while entranced by the ideas behind his project as well as the story itself, I felt that the text as it was written was inaccessible. As clever and witty as Gozzi's barbs against Goldoni may have been in his own time, the parody of figures long forgotten would simply be lost to today's audience. The dialogue outlined in the scenario, relying heavily on the humor of the parody, was overly simplistic and disjointed, relying on the talent of the actors to help it to flow.

While browsing through information on Gozzi and Goldoni, however, I stumbled upon an inspired idea. For Gozzi, his project around *TLOTO* was only partially for commercial success. Mainly he was making an intellectual statement about what he saw as ineffectual trends in his contemporary theatre and personifying his personal beliefs about theatricality in the characters on stage. Thus a very simple plan began to occur to me: Could I perform a comedic experiment by recreating Gozzi's project today? What if I was to rewrite Gozzi's scenario into a full play text, only this time with my own agenda for reform and contemporary parody substituted in for the dated elements of his?

Gozzi had several main issues with Goldoni and his contemporaries that he singled out in *TLOTO*. Predominately, he objected to the tainting of the Italian language (most specifically Gozzi felt they copied the French and Voltaire) and the style of Martellian verse.

My rewrite of *TLOTO* hinges on three main changes. The first was simply smoothing out the dialogue and characters, to develop some of the parts further and to fix the flow of the narrative within the scenes. Since the scenes were written out in paragraph form, I wanted to fill in actual lines for my cast of non-commedia actors (as most troupes are today), and writing out the dialogue gave me a greater control over the comic elements that went into the play.

The second largest change involved the many parodies and invocations of Martellian verse. Though references to this form appeared all over the original text, I removed all of them since they would be lost on a modern audience. The spells of Morgana and Celio, originally written in a parody of this style, became nursery rhyme style poems while the "horrors" of Creonta exchanged their Martellian verse for a parody of Shakespeare ("Fakespeare"). The nursery rhyme spells seemed to fit with the fairy tale theme of the play while the parodies of Shakespeare carried the flavor of Gozzi's original joke in a way that is still accessible to the average audience member. The last of the horrors, the gate, spoke in a very modern street slang because, while also very funny in its incongruity, that slang has become a modern language style so defined it is almost equivalent to something as formalized as verse.

The largest change Gozzi's story received in my hands however, had to do with a seemingly simple change that effectively altered the timbre of the entire production. Gozzi's prologue, a plea for the revitalization of commedia, is meant to be spoken by one of the troupe, out of character. This character, listed as the Speaker of the Prologue, essentially won over the audience before the play itself was sent on stage.

Exactly what to do with this Prologue plagued me and I even debated cutting it out entirely as my agenda was so different from Gozzi's. In the end, I decided to alter the speech to be a summary of my project and even toyed with the idea of delivering it myself as the director/playwright before the performance. As I also considered what actor could play double duty and perform this large speech, I made perhaps the largest decision of the rewrite. The character of Celio, the good magician, (almost a throw away character in the original version because he is a parody of Goldoni and essentially only functions as that) became the Narrator of the entire play.

This allowed for several interesting things to occur. Firstly, it gave the character of Celio far more weight as he was not only a powerful wizard but also held control over the very direction of the narrative itself. It also allowed him to deliver the Prologue as a member of the cast itself, pleading on behalf of the characters of giving this old story a new chance, while also unifying the action of the play with his commentary and continued presence.

Celio also took a more active role in the plot with this change as he is on stage for nearly every scene and this allowed him direct control over the outcome of things. Perhaps the best example of this is when Tartaglia laughs and the first curse is broken. Though in the original scenario Celio is indirectly responsible for this since he sends Truffaldino to the court, the Narrator/Celio is not only present at the ball itself; he is also the one who trips Morgana, not Truffaldino.

As a playwright, I knew this tactic of adding a Narrator had succeeded when, one of the nights of performance, Celio re-entered to stop Morgana in the nick of time and his entrance was greeted with loud and excited applause. Suddenly, Gozzi's parody play was not just a collection of buffoons and had begun to feature sympathetic characters. But more importantly, it apparently now had a hero.

The addition of the Narrator also allowed for other moments of potential as other characters interacted with him, referenced him and even kidnapped him to tell the story their own way. But more importantly, it paved the way for other characters to also break that precarious fourth wall. An important distinction between Gozzi's play and my own is this: mine features characters in a story while his was actors in a play. Though seemingly a small difference, the addition of the

Narrator in this version established ground rules that, while actors may address the audience, they are never out of character. (Even in the curtain call, I had them bow in character, something which unified the play perfectly.)

There is something latently comic in the reflexive properties this narrator construct opened up and it furnished me with an excellent opportunity to utilize this phenomena. Such intrusions through the fourth wall unhinge the members of the audience and tapping into this surprise will reward the performer with many laughs. However, with the actors holding to their characters, even with them breaking the fourth wall and directly relating to the audience, the audience was never distanced in any Brechtian way from the action and was hopefully more likely to forgive these departures since the reality of the characters remained intact.

~

In the end, I would have to say that my project was a success. What this text accomplishes is two-fold, for, while a funny and solid play in its own right, it is also true in many ways to the principles that Gozzi held it to. The difference is that this time, a reader today can get the same sense of the text that the playwright intended, without having the comedy bogged down by footnotes.

~Hillary DePiano

Table of Contents

Production Notes

The following are suggestions, tips, hints and
warnings about performing this play.

Setting

For the original production of this play,
Guerry Hood designed a raised platform with
ramps leading up to it which was the basis
for all scenes. It was painted as such that
it could look like indoors or outdoors
depending on the lighting of the scene. The
backdrop of all scenes was a large book, made
to look like a dusty antique volume with the
title written on the front in gold. The play
began with the book closed and then the
narrator would turn the "pages" on his
narration before each scene. Each page was a
painted flat of the background of that scene.
For simplicity's sake, our production used
only a general inside palace room for all
scenes in the palace, a general outside scene
of the forest, the inside of Morgana's
castle, and Creonta's yard. After Creonta's,
the narrator began to turn the book backwards
(i.e., two pages at once to get back to the
forest and then back to the palace for the
final scene). This way, when it came time for
him to close the book at the end of the
curtain call, it was only one page thick and
thus much faster and easier to turn.

For all forest scenes, we had a large
signpost (for hiding behind, able to be
turned in many directions depending on which
way the characters were coming from) and a
log large enough for all three oranges to sit
on at once. These were moved around the
forest alternately depending on the scene to
denote different parts of the woods.

Musician/Music

An unseen presence who furnishes his commentary on the scenes with music from vaudeville to the soap opera, he has a tendency to pad his part. This can be anything from a single person with a keyboard to a small band or even canned musical effects. It is, however, preferable if the musician is real person. Not only does this allow for the musician to perform live, adjusting to the performance as it happens, but it also gives the music a personality of its own and makes its appearances in the story less environmental and more like an impish comment on the action when it appears. Our performances utilized a single keyboardist who performed from the booth, but was hidden from the audience by a black mesh. While he was not seen, he still interacted with the characters in the places indicated and was able to reflect the intensity, foibles and pace of the actors in his music as he was essentially one of them.

He is in direct contact with the Narrator at all times, while the other characters only acknowledge him when he is particularly obtrusive.

Improvisation

Improvisation, while such an integral element of Gozzi's original text, here provides some pitfalls. The scenes most designed to be extemporaneous such as the chases and fights are the most dangerous to be done so. While improvisation is encouraged in the rehearsal process, ensure that the action of your chases and fights is set by dress rehearsals to minimize injury to the performers.

Puppets

There is a good deal of potential for puppet use throughout the production. Preferably, the actress playing Ninetta performs the dove puppet herself which allows the audience to see the emotions of the dove as they play out on the actress's face. Her transformation is simply tossing the dove aside when she becomes a princess again.

Besides the obvious opportunities with the donkey, gate and rope, the first production also included hobby horses that served as Tartaglia and Truffaldino's steeds on their quest. The actors mounted them and rode them as if they were real horses and manipulated like puppets both while riding and after dismounting to make them seem alive. This also provided some extra comedy for, once the convention is established, while Tartaglia keeps with it, Truffaldino abandons it and exits the forest scene with the horse in a bag slung over his shoulder.

The Love of
Three Oranges

List of Characters

Narrator

Silvio, King of Hearts, dressed like the playing card

Pantalone, adviser to the King

Leandro, First Minister

Princess Clarice, niece to the King

Brighella, Leandro and Clarice's dimwitted minion

Prince Tartaglia, Jack of Hearts, when formal, he is dressed like the playing card

Truffaldino, a famous jester, employed by Celio

Smeraldina, Fata Morgana's slightly less dimwitted minion

Fata Morgana, an evil witch

Farfarello, a unionized devil

The Wind God, loyal to Fata Morgana

A gate, of unspeakable horror

A donkey, of unutterable horror

A rope, of horror that cannot possibly be spoken

A cook, of about average horror

Creonta, another evil witch

Princess Ninetta, formerly an orange

Princess Nicoletta, also formerly an orange

Princess Linetta, yet another former orange

Musician, unseen presence who furnishes his commentary on the scenes with music from vaudeville to the soap opera

Assorted country bumpkins, palace guards, servants, and feast guests

PLACE: *A fairy tale Kingdom*

TIME: *The time is the imaginary present.*

Prologue

[The play begins with the house lights on so the audience can be seated. A giant book with "The Love of Three Oranges" written on the cover is on the stage, which will serve as the backdrop for each scene to come. It is closed. There is no curtain covering the stage. A minute after the curtain time, the Narrator runs onto the stage rather frazzled. He is wearing an ordinary suit and tie. His eyes scan the crowd in a bit of a panic. He begins, quietly at first, to try to get the audience's attention. The lights do not go out in the house until he decides to begin the play after his speech]

Rush 2 C. (Nervous)

NARRATOR: Ladies and gentlemen! Excuse me! Can I have your attention please? Thank you. I'm sorry, but it seems we have a situation on our hands. You see, right now, all the characters that make up this story are hiding on the other side of these curtains. They know their parts. They're dressed and ready, but still they refuse to come out. And quite honestly it's because they are scared. They are afraid they will bore you. They suspect you've figured out by now that this is a commedia play and are edging towards the door. They think you would rather watch TV or go to the movies or at least see a play that is new, modern and critically acclaimed, rather than hear a story as old and musty as theirs.

You must understand our position! It's so hard to find a tale that pleases you! Your tastes move with the wind and we can't predict where they will go next. A story that met with huge success back then is now met with projectile vegetation. We only know that we have hit our mark when we hear you laugh or applaud our efforts and that is all the reward we need.

[Beginning to get rather frustrated] Today's plots are so above our heads. They have so many layers, characters, twists and turns. And they also have to be philosophical, rich, edgy, symbolic, dense, fat and full of surprises, sex, religion, feminism, race, violence, orientation, profanity and social commentary. We leave these looking at one another in confusion and terror. Where do we fit into this fray? "Comedy is so low brow," they say. "Theatre is only for the elite," they say. "It can't win an award if it's only a comedy!" they say! *[Sigh. Resigned.]* Perhaps you have a point. Our story has been told since before any of you were born and in a world that devours the new and immediate, I suppose our simple old tale can't compete. *[Begins to walk off stage. Downtrodden. Kicks ground. On second thought. Starts back]*

But on behalf of all the characters in this story, I swear that we would give our eyeteeth, digits, or gallbladders to win your love and devotion! They would have wanted me to assure you of this from the start and I do so with all my heart. We will try anything to please you. We have no pride, no reservations, nothing to keep us from amusing you. If we were concerned about looking foolish, we would be sitting out there with you and not down here dressed like clowns. So our only choice is to do our best and hope that even if you find us

untalented, you will laugh at that and
it will be good enough for us.

You know us already! We've been here all along
     in the sketch comedy, the spoofs, and
     the sitcom. You've met us before by a
     million different names and faces. Try
     to remember! We don't understand why we
     fell out of your favor, for it wasn't
     all that long ago that you preferred us
     to the intellectual barrage of the artsy
     fartsy. You used to treat us so
     graciously, yet now so many of our kind
     are unemployed, lying idle between the
     pages of dusty unread books and cast
     aside with other fads and trends. Some
     of us seldom see the light of day and
     when we do it is in the study of some
     crusty theatre scholar, a classroom, or
     some poor fool writing a thesis. What
     ever happened to the merits of a good
     story? Is it the jokes? The language?
     Aren't we hip? Is it right
     that Harlequin and the Macarana lie in
     the same grave?

Just give us a chance to make this story new
     and reborn. You no sooner throw out your
     ghastly day glow bell bottoms when, lo,
     they are back in style and twice as
     expensive. So do not be so quick to
     judge our time as spent, we may surprise
     you yet. In the face of so much horror,
     the constant threat of war, suffering,
     and the world weighing down on us, I
     refuse to believe there is no place for
     laughter! We will not fade away! Levity
     is what saves us from the load and you
     can keep it all from reality TV to the
     daily news but we will continue in our
     staunch crusade to prove that there is
     and will always be room in this world
     for amusement simply for amusement's

sake! What do you say? Will you laugh with us in the face of reality and tell the world to get over itself?

You will witness many strange things this evening and we ask you to please check your disbelief at the door of the theatre. I'm sure your humble servants, the characters that make up this tale, will be ready to begin as soon as they hear you call for them. Your applause and laughter is the life that courses through their veins and once they hear your willingness to give them a chance, it will wipe out all their initial reservations. So, are you willing to give our old story a new chance? ~~[he encourages them to clap. The characters being to peek tentatively out of the curtains at the sound. To the Light booth.~~] So, can we please have the lights down some? Excellent. First I'd like to tell you what the story is about, but I'm a little afraid you'll laugh at me. Because the story is . . . *[unsure of what to say]* well it's mostly about oranges . . . and happiness . . . and a little about love. Maybe you should just see for yourself. So just sit back like you were a little child on your grandfather's knee and let me tell you a story like you have never heard before.

[As he says this final line, he turns and opens the book to the backdrop of the castle. He claps once to signal the beginning. Chaos as characters begin to emerge from all sides pushing scenery and carrying props, costumes and other actors, bumping into each other in their excitement to begin the show. The three girls, who later play the oranges (in their Act 1 costumes, NOT the oranges outfits) skip

across the stage hand-in-hand. Some of the actors preset the frozen King and Pantalone and position them for the scene. During the madness, the Narrator stops Truffaldino and whispers to him for a moment. He points out Tartaglia to him and then the two part, Truffaldino to offstage, the Narrator to the audience where he takes a seat to watch. No other character acknowledges the Narrator as anything more than an obstacle in their path. They set up for the first scene and clear the stage and the Narrator claps to signal for them to begin.]

End of Prologue

ACT I

Act 1, Scene I

[a room in the palace. King Silvio, Pantalone, and guards.]

SILVIO, KING OF HEARTS: Oh, Pantalone, advisor to me, the King! My only son, Tartaglia, sole heir to my throne, is still sick after all these months. He lies in his room day in and day out, too ill to leave, miserable and dying and yet we still do not know what has made him so sick. Meanwhile, on a potentially unrelated note, Princess Clarice, second in the line of succession to the throne, grows more strange and cruel by the moment. Now the doctors have said that there is no hope for recovery and the kingdom is as good as destroyed. Oh, the inhumanity! *[King sobs]*

PANTALONE: This is true, but with all due respect, your Majesty, why are you telling me this? Perhaps you have forgotten but I live here. I know all this already.

KING: Oh, I know.

PANTALONE: Then . . .why. . ?

KING: It's for them. *[Points to the audience]* Plot exposition.

PANTALONE: Ah! Very good your majesty. Very clever. It was interwoven so well I hardly noticed.

KING: That's why I'm King. *[In a daze]* I still do not understand where he could have gotten such a sickness. I've always made him wear his coat outdoors and wash his hands before eating and I never let him kiss frogs. . .

PANTALONE: Your majesty. *[Pantalone signals to the King to come closer and he says confidentially]* I don't mean to be indiscreet, but could the illness be something that you *[chooses word]* contracted in your youth?

KING: Pardon? I'm not following.

PANTALONE: What I mean to say sire, is that you may have *[chooses word]* known several women other than the Queen. . .

KING: Good God man! Why are you whispering? *[loudly]* Nothing to be ashamed of. Lord, Pantalone, I knew women at an early age. I had all my sisters and I showed my aunts a good time as soon as I was able to walk. And to say nothing of my Grandmother! Ah the times that bathtub has seen. I was dirty and grandma would rub me down. Oh, the games we played in that tub! I had her squealing after a few seconds and she had me done in less than 5 minutes. And my mother, allow me to tell you sir, that there are few people who have the sort of relationship with their mother that I had. Many a night I kept her up, screaming. This one time. . .

PANTALONE: Your majesty! Stop speaking please your highness! *[A glance to the guards who tuned in just at the wrong time. He returns to whispering.]* What I am trying to say is, perhaps your snake caught something when it wandered into a strange jungle. . .

KING: Can't say that I've ever had a snake. I'm much more of a cat person. . . *[Suddenly understands.]* Oh! *[Answer to the unspoken question]* No. I have always been faithful, completely faithful, to my wife, the Queen. May she rest in peace.

PANTALONE: Hmm. Well, let's not underestimate the prince. Maybe he got a dose himself.

KING: *[King shakes his head no]* Prince Tartaglia has never known love. *[sappy music]* He is still waiting for someone or something to animate his heart. *[music stops abruptly]* No, Pantalone. I have had him examined by all the greatest doctors in the land and for once they all agree.

PANTALONE: And what do they agree it is?

KING: It is an extremely grave, and most probably fatal, case of *[big dramatic pause]* terminal hypochondria. *[dramatic flourish of music]*

PANTALONE: Hypochondria?

KING: Yes! The doctors say there is nothing they can do to cure him. They say that the only thing that might cure him is to make him laugh! The best we can do is try to improve his spirits in the hope that it will make him well. Oh, my poor child. My only son! Just a little smile on his face would be a sign of an improvement. But it is impossible. Ah, it grieves me, Pantalone. I'm such an old man, already quite decrepit, and my only son lies on his deathbed, which means that the crown will pass to my niece, Princess Clarice, who just generally creeps me out. Death by hypochondria! *[The King weeps again.]*

PANTALONE: There, there sire. Stop grieving like this or you'll be on your deathbed too. You'll never get the prince to laugh with this kind of behavior! There is hope in what you said. We are in luck! By chance, or some cheap plot set-up, the great comedian Truffaldino has arrived at the court today. Why, how do you expect to get the prince to laugh when the whole court is in mourning! What I suggest is... Have a party! We'll have games and a tournament! It could be a masked ball! With all the merriment of the costumes and feast, the prince is bound to at least chuckle. I'll bet Truffaldino, if anyone, can cure the prince of this terminal hypochondrium. Can it hurt?

KING: Hmmm. There is something in what you say...

PANTALONE: What have you got to lose? We've tried everything else!

KING: But the boy is sick! All the noise and festivities might make him worse.

PANTALONE: But sick with hypochondria!

KING: Terminal hypochondria. Yes . . . *[not getting it]*

PANTALONE: That means it is all in his mind!

KING: Hmmm.... Well, I'll try it. I will go see Truffaldino immediately. Order a banquet for the whole court! *[Leandro enters.]*

PANTALONE: *[aside to audience]* That's Leandro, the First Minister. I don't trust him at all. I'll bet he wants the prince dead.

LEANDRO: *[aside to audience]* Hi! I'm Leandro, the First Minister. Boy, do I want the prince dead.

KING: Ah, Leandro, I was just about to give orders for some festivities. We are having a court banquet and a masked ball with entertainment for the prince starring the great clown Truffaldino and we are having it tonight. I also hereby decree that whoever can make the prince laugh, by whatever means, will get a huge prize.

LEANDRO: But your Majesty, is this wise? I beg you, reconsider these orders, for poor Prince Tartaglia is a very sick man. Such activity could easily cause his death.

KING: Leandro, everything else we have tried from magicians to magnets has failed to cure the prince. Laughter cannot possibly hurt him, at the very least. I myself will go to the kitchen and order a royal banquet for the whole court. Ah, Pantalone, you have given me new hope!

PANTALONE: *[sucking up]* Well, actually, your majesty, it was mostly your idea.

KING: Was it? So, that's why I'm king.

PANTALONE: Oh, your highness, you are such a card.

KING: Shut up Pantalone. *[The King and Pantalone exit quickly, followed by the guards.]*

LEANDRO: *[calls after them]* Your highness, I beg you to reconsider! This is a foolish, hasty move that will not help a sick boy get better. *[they are gone]* Damn that meddling Pantalone! And where did this insipid clown Truffaldino come from? If the prince laughs even once then all our efforts will be for nothing. ARG! Why hasn't the infernal whiner died yet? Who is interfering with our plans?

[Princess Clarice enters and runs to Leandro. She is the princess, flighty and used to always getting her way. Leandro needs her in order to get to the throne, but otherwise has little use for her.]

CLARICE: Oh, my most precious! Love you! Kisses! Cheek! Cheek! Lips! Fish face!

LEANDRO: *[begrudgingly complies with the tired routine]* Shnookums, perhaps we should not be so free with affections until the prince is dead.

CLARICE: *[pouts]* O foo. OK. But I am tired of waiting. I want to get married now. Why can't we just shoot him or slit his throat or something classic like that? Why do we have to use such an unnecessarily slow and complex death?

LEANDRO: Patience, my little peachy blossom. This is just how things are done. *[under his breath]* As I tell you all the damn time, *[out loud]* I have enlisted a very powerful ally, one who will begin to tip the balance.

CLARICE: Oh yeah! *[pause]* Who is it again?

LEANDRO: That pillar of evil, that spokesperson of treachery, that paragon of all things that are just generally not that nice. It is Fata Morgana, *[chord]* a powerful sorceress whose very name brings fear to the ears that speak it. *[from this point in the play on, a chord occurs after anyone says "Fata Morgana"]*

CLARICE: Ears that speak it?

LEANDRO: *[ignores her]* Of course the doctors think he is faking! It is through Morgana's magic potions that the prince has fallen ill and it will be her magic that finishes him off and allows her to finally get her revenge!

CLARICE: Oh, pookie! You're so sexy when you're colluding.

LEANDRO: And then, when the prince is dead, I will marry you and then I will be King!

CLARICE: And I will be Queen!

LEANDRO: *[slightly overlapping her line]* With me as King! *[they begin a full bodied evil laugh and freeze mid laugh when the Narrator suddenly claps]*

NARRATOR: Time Out! *[he walks in silence to the frozen pair and chuckles at them.]* Would you look at them? That can't be comfortable to hold for a long time. *[tickles LEANDRO under the chin]* Koochy koochy koo. *[laughs at himself and ends with a "hoo" end of laugh kind of sigh. He looks at the audience for a moment with no idea why they are all looking at him so expectantly]* Oh, right! Sorry to interrupt the flow of things but I just wanted to fill you in. You see, Fata Morgana, *[chord]* this evil witch our frozen chums were just talking about, always loved a good game of cards. She loved it because she always won. She always won because she always cheated. But one day, while playing with another witch who was simply a better cheater, Morgana lost 2 of her best brooms when she was miserably defeated. The game? *[musical build up]* Hearts. *[dramatic flourish of music]* So it was this slight that made Morgana hire the bandits that killed the Queen of Hearts years ago and made her run over the King's royal cat, Ace, with an ice cream truck last May. This is also what fuels her endless desire for revenge now. She will not rest until she has destroyed the King and his son as well. ~~[he begins to make his way back to his seat as he finishes his speech]~~ I just wanted to fill you in on a little of the background info. Things will begin to go much smoother now that we've gotten most of this expositional crap out of the way. ~~[sits and then claps, bringing them back to life. They fall immediately out of their laughter poses and begin looking at the sky in all directions.]~~

LEANDRO: What the hell was that?

CLARICE: Owie. Why do I feel so stiff?

LEANDRO: Someone or something is interfering. Guiding things along their own way. I don't like it. First that Truffaldino shows up out of nowhere.

CLARICE: OOOOO! I like him! He's very funny!

LEANDRO: *[losing his patience]* Which, my little love bucket, is the problem! The doctors are right about one thing, if Tartaglia laughs, even once, Morgana's spell will be broken and I will never be King.

CLARICE: Then I will never be Queen.

LEANDRO: *[overlap]* Or I King. The only thing more discouraging than the appearance of this buffoon is the King's sudden whim of having a ball. Oh, Morgana is not going to be pleased.

[BRIGHELLA runs in]

BRIGHELLA: Master! Boy is Morgana ever pissed! I just saw her henchwoman, Smeraldina. The clown's appearance and the idea for the banquet were both planted by Celio, the good magician, and Morgana's most bitter rival. The two have never met on this earth, but he has foiled Morgana's plans for years and she vows to destroy him. He's the one who sent Truffaldino here to break the spell and to protect the prince and King. *cue*

NARRATOR: *(clap)* [claps his hands. Everyone freezes. To audience.] You getting all this? [claps his hands again and the scene continues] → *(clap)*

CLARICE: So, let's kill the jester! Quickly! I have a gun in my room and a few knives.
. .

LEANDRO: No. No. We shall use more magic potions from Morgana.

CLARICE: [sarcastic] Oh, they worked sooooo well on the Prince. That was a nice speedy death. [LEANDRO looks as though he is about to attack. Brighella separates them.]

BRIGHELLA: My lord and lady! Calm yourselves! Fata Morgana [chord] herself will be here tonight for the festivities. She will finish off Truffaldino once and for all and make sure the prince never laughs. She sends word to double the amount of poison you slip into his medicine today and to rest assured and attend the party as if nothing was amiss, for if he does not laugh tonight, he will be dead by morning.

CLARICE: Well that would be wonderful.

BRIGHELLA: *[Hannibal Lector]* Hello Clarice.

CLARICE: Could you please not do that? It really freaks me out.

LEANDRO: Come. We must go and plan for tonight. *[begins to exit. The others pause]*

BRIGHELLA: With all due respect, sir, didn't we just plan for tonight?

CLARICE: Yeah, that's what I thought we were doing.

LEANDRO: True. *[a pause. Then, exactly as before]* Come. Let us get off the stage so that the next scene can get on... *[He exits.]*

BRIGHELLA: *[to CLARICE]* That works. *[she shrugs in agreement and the two exit]*

Act 1, Scene 2

[The hypochondriacal prince's bedchamber. Prince Tartaglia himself is carried onto the stage, frozen mid-sneeze. He is covered by a ridiculously large blanket pulled up to his neck, with an ice pack on his head and a huge thermometer in his mouth which he takes out and checks occasionally during the scene. There is an I.V. with two bags on an I.V. stand attached to his arm. Next to the chair is a table piled with medicine bottles, ointments, salves, pills, spittoons, hot water bottles, and other medical paraphernalia. The narrator, who has turned the page during the set-up, walks across the stage.]

Center

NARRATOR: Meanwhile, on the opposite side of the castle, unaware of the plots against him, Prince Tartaglia was in misery. Though whether it was from the potions of Morgana or his own outlook, I leave you to decide. *[claps]*

X to chair

PRINCE TARTAGLIA: *[unfreezes into a big sneeze. Sad music plays. Elaborate show of blowing his nose.]* Poor me! *[He coughs.]* What a fate! I've tried everything. Acupuncture, herbal remedies, even TV evangelists. *[ala faith healer]* I felt the power! I have my crystals and magnets. I even tried that drinking my own pee business. Yet I'm always weak, always sick, and always *[he coughs pathetically]*... sad. *[Sad music fades out. His watch beeps]* Oh! It's time for my medicine, *[He lovingly takes a spoonful of something out of one of the bottles. Savors it like a connoisseur.]* Mmmm . . . It tastes like crap, but at least I feel a little

better. But my head still hurts. I get
fainting spells and dizzy spells and
Speak N' spells. I always have a fever
and my joints hurt. I also get hot
flashes and sometimes hot flushes - one
rises from the feet and the other goes
down from the head. I need an enema at
least once a week to keep my bowels
regular. Otherwise, I'm blocked up for
days.

[Truffaldino enters like the announcer in a
boxing match. He acts out the boxing match,
playing all of the parts himself with the
boxers on either side and the announcer in the
center]

TRUFFALDINO: [as   announcer]   Ladies   and
gentlemen, allow me to welcome you to
the bout of the century! In the left
corner we have the pure bulk and
destructive power of the returning
champion! [as Champ]   UNG! I'm the
champ! Watch out! I'm gonna eat your
children! [Announcer] And in the right
corner we have an elderly British woman.
[Terrified British woman]   Oh please
gov'ner, take care! [Announcer begins
fight]   Let's get it on! [Bell sounds.
as Champ warming up and shadowboxing]
Show me what you got. Show me what you
got! [British woman who mimes taking out
a purse]   Oh, I only have about four
pounds and twenty quid. [Confused Champ]
That's not really what I meant lady.
[British woman sighs dejectedly]   Very
well then. [She suddenly pulls arm back
to punch champ with all her might.
Truffaldino then jumps over and plays
the champ taking the hit in the face and
falling over comically, unconscious. He
then jumps back up, bows and works the
crowd before confidently returning to

see the effect of this on the still stoic Prince] Funny?

TARTAGLIA: No.

TRUFFALDINO: *[Truffaldino is momentarily annoyed but then begins again.]* Very well. I don't usually use my A material on charity cases, but for you I will make an exception. *[He surveys the situation and then rips the I.V. out of Tartaglia's arm and ignoring the Prince's yelp of pain, takes center stage. The rest of the stage darkens and a spotlight hits him. As he begins this next bit of dialogue, he begins to extend the I.V. stand as high as it will go and use it as a microphone.]* Maestro, if you please. *[The introduction to "Send in the Clowns" begins]* Ladies and gentlemen, what I have for you now is a story about a couple of people that just met. One of them is giving the other a bit of trouble but let's see if they can get through in the end. *[Truffaldino then sings an abridged version of "Send in the Clowns" working the crowd whenever possible, using the tube as the microphone wire and waving/winking to fans and friends in the audience. He sings "Isn't it rich, are we a pair?/Me here at last on the ground, you in mid air!/Send in the clowns!/Quick! Send in the clowns!/Don't bother I'm here!" The last line is his big finish and he begins to squeeze the IV bags tightly as he hits his final note. As he squeezes them, he begins to look at them and their positioning. He grabs these new "breasts" and notices that one bag is much larger than the other. To the audience]* Excuse me, doc, but aren't these supposed to be the same size? *[The* *lights come up and he returns triumphantly to the prince to find him still un-amused. In frustration he contemplates one of the I. V. bags and then pretends to throw it at the prince.]* Think fast! *[This also gets no reaction from the prince.]* Oh give me a break. Not even a tiny bit funny?

TARTAGLIA: *[whines]* No! It was loud and boring. It gave me a hives and athletes foot. And since you've been here I think I am developing dandruff. Who the hell are you anyway?

TRUFFALDINO: Who am I? I am the internationally famous clown and wandering court jester, Truffaldino. I'm the father of farce. The lord of laughter. The sultan of shtick. I'm your stand up comedian, your slapstick cartoon hero, and the soul of commedia dell'arte all blended together with a dash of pizzazz and a bit of old school goofiness for a milk shake of comedic delight. Only now that I think of it, I'm not really that much like a milk shake because that is cold and I, your hypochondriacal highness, am red hot! I make everyone laugh.

TARTAGLIA: Well you don't make me laugh. Don't quit your day job just yet. *[turns over as if he is going to sleep]*

TRUFFALDINO: *[makes motion like he going to strangle Tartaglia. Narrator clears his throat loudly. Truffaldino hears him, checks himself and composes himself.]* Let me feel your pulse. Just as I thought. Normal.

TARTAGLIA: It is NOT normal! My throat hurts and I *[he starts coughing]*... phlegm! ... phlegm! ... I have to spit... quick, get the... *[Truffaldino gets the spittoon for him; the prince spits into it. Truffaldino examines the contents of the spittoon.]*

TRUFFALDINO: Oh, that was lovely. *[Sounds of music and people talking and laughing are heard offstage.]* Do you hear that your highness? They are having a ball and festival in your honor! Wouldn't you like to go?

TARTAGLIA: A festival, eh? No way in hell. A festival in my condition? I'm a very sick man and have to stay in bed near my medicines. My precious . . . *[Tartaglia hugs his medicine bottles to him. Truffaldino looks ready to give up and gestures to the narrator that the situation is hopeless. The narrator indicates that Truffaldino will have his throat cut if he does not comply. So Truffaldino, now much more aggressive and no longer pussy footing around, begins to throw the medicine bottles off stage]*

TARTAGLIA: Are you crazy? What are you doing? Stop! Stop, you lunatic! My medicines! Stop! I'll die without my medicines!

[Chase music. He frantically begins to try to retrieve the bottles. When he stands Truffaldino takes the blanket and hot compress from his head and throws them off stage. Truffaldino holds the last of the medicine, Tartaglia runs for it. They chase. This chase takes them through the audience and

*Truffaldino may even elicit the help of an
audience member to hide the bottle for a
while. He finally tricks the prince and
catches him and, swinging the prince over his
shoulder, he carries him kicking and whining
offstage.]*

TRUFFALDINO: Frankly, your highness, I don't
      give a damn. You are going to the
      banquet if it kills one of us.

TARTAGLIA: Stop! Stop! I'll die! I'm too sick
      to go out! Where's my air purifier?
      Stop! Stop...

*[Exit. The whole time Tartaglia is yelling and
      crying pathetically.]*

Act 1, Scene 3

[Narrator turns the page to a court room in the palace. A few assorted people put finishing touches on the decorations. Light music plays underneath. The Narrator oversees the scene change and then says to the audience:]

NARRATOR: And so it was time for the royal costume ball and the kingdom prepared, throwing together the most elaborate and ornate costumes they could find, all hoping to make the prince laugh and save the kingdom. Tartaglia's illness had all but outlawed happiness in the kingdom and this chance to break free from the kingdom-wide mourning and cut loose created a feeling of hope and joy in everyone. And I do mean everyone. *[he unbuttons some of his shirt to reveal a costume underneath, smiles, and then exits the stage. Leandro enters and begins to pace downstage of those that are decorating]*

LEANDRO: Well, I have carried out the King's orders. He decreed that there would be a banquet, a masked ball, and entertainments this very night and I have made it so. The people are preparing comical costumes to make the prince laugh but I will ensure that our costumes remind him only of death and depress him more. *[Fata Morgana, hunched over and dressed as a ridiculous old hag, enters and tries to walk past him.]* Just a sec, grandma. Where do you think you are going? The party hasn't even started yet.

FATA MORGANA: *[smacks him and stands her full height.]* Fool. Don't you recognize me? It is I, *[She throws her hood back to reveal her face. She is a very powerful, sexy woman.]* Fata Morgana *[chord]* and I'm here to help you, for as long as I am present in this room, the prince will never laugh. And if he does not laugh, he does not live! And if he does not live, he dies! *[a pause as she realizes that was rather lame]* Grovel!

LEANDRO: *[getting on his knees and kissing her hand]* My Queen, my benefactor, my most holy rolling stone! I did not recognize you in your costume, but I am thankful for your supernatural help.

FATA MORGANA: That's more like it. Smeraldina, my loyal henchwoman! Help me with this hood thing. *[Smeraldina enters and helps her back into her old lady costume. Morgana resumes her bent position Leandro is still groveling with fear.]* What the hell are you waiting for simpleton? Open the doors and let the party begin.

[Fata Morgana retreats to the back of the room as the guests file in. Clarice enters with Leandro's costume. Both her and Leandro are dressed in costumes to remind the prince of death. Fanfare. Flourish. Silvio, Truffaldino and Prince Tartaglia enter, the father and son in full playing card regalia. Tartaglia looks perfectly miserable and tries several times to escape but Truffaldino is right behind. Some guests stop Truffaldino for his autograph and the Prince escapes but runs into Pantalone on his way out, only to have the clown bring him back. The King and Prince sit on their thrones. They eventually have to tie the

prince to the chair and gag him to get him to stay. As they are tying up the prince, Brighella enters wearing his usual costume and the mask from "Scream." This gets a big reaction from Clarice and Leandro who are at first scared but also show their approval. Among the guests is the narrator dressed similar to Where's Waldo. Everyone is in some sort of mask for this scene as a little send up to old school commedia.]

Enter as Waldo

KING: *[addresses entire audience]* Ah beloved subjects, welcome! We are here tonight in pursuit of happiness. Most specifically, the happiness of my only son, Prince Tartaglia. Whoever can make him laugh will get this huge sack of gold. Though I say now *[sappy music]* that if you can touch his heart and make him happy, truly happy, my kingdom is yours. *[music stops]* But for now, a laugh will do. Let the entertainments begin. *[Truffaldino begins to gather the guests and assign them roles in the joust.]*

TRUFFALDINO: All right let's get this show rolling. Entertainment number one, a joust!

[The Narrator hands the 'squires' Truffaldino appointed their lances and they become different characters immediately. They touch the 'challengers' and they too become their roles. The challengers then each touch one other who gets down on all fours. The challengers face off at opposite sides of the stage with their squires and horses. Truffaldino signals for the rest of the guests to make a drum roll and then begins to search for something in his pockets.]

KING: The coin toss! *[Truffaldino finally finds what he is looking for, but instead of a coin, it is a rubber chicken. He lifts it high above his head.]*

LEANDRO: *[aside]* Oh crap. This guy is good.

[Truffaldino uses the chicken as the coin and does the coin toss into the audience. After consulting with the audience member it landed on or near to determine the outcome, he shouts out the result and announces that this means the joust will be on foot. Sadly the two "horses" get up and walk dejectedly to the sides of the stage. They each snort sadly. He begins the joust. Challenger 1 is a very aggressive and confident fighter. She/he is always flexing, working the crowd and showing his/her teeth to the other challenger. This works best if this challenger is played by someone small and petite, perhaps one of the actresses that later play the princesses. Challenger #2, however, is terrified of the idea of the fight and keeps trying to hide behind his/her squire. #1's squire tosses the lance to him/her and #1 catches it. The crowd is impressed. #2's squire begins to toss the lance but #2 only cowers in fear. The crowd is disappointed. #2's squire finally hands #2 the lance and he/she hands it directly back. The squire begins to walk away, realizes the switch and finally firmly hands the lance to #2 horizontally at chest level. #2 takes it and turns around quickly, nearly hitting the squire who ducks quickly under it. #1 advances, lance ready. #2 holds the lance like a baseball bat. The crowd laughs. #2 sees #1 and adjusts the lance the same way. The crowd cheers. #2 is rather pleased and turns around 180 degrees quickly, assuming he/she is done, forcing everyone nearby to quickly swerve or duck to avoid the tip of his/her lance.

*Finally Truffaldino shouts "Jousters Ready?"
Once the joust begins, everyone on stage with
the exception of Prince Tartaglia goes into
slow motion. The Musician plays "Chariots of
Fire." Prince Tartaglia still moves in real
time, looking at the others on stage with
confusion. The jousters charge and run right
past each other. They turn around for another
pass and on the way back, #1 accidentally
stabs Truffaldino. Then #2 stabs his other
side. The jousters run out of the way and
Truffaldino drops the rubber chicken and then
begins to fall. Then everyone goes back into
real time and is shocked/horrified that
Truffaldino has been killed. He then removes
the lances, uses them as ski poles and the
crowd laughs with joy and relief that he is
fine.]*

TRUFFALDINO: [*aside to the King*] Did he laugh?

KING: [*removing Tartaglia's gag*] Wasn't that funny!

TARTAGLIA: [*shouting*] No. Not at all. I can't breathe, the air is so stuffy in here, and all this noise is giving me a headache. Please, Daddy, can't I just go back to my nice warm bed. I need my medicines. And all the bacteria and microbes in this room are no good for . . . [*the King shoves the gag back into his mouth*]

KING: [*aside to Truffaldino*] No. He seems worse.

TRUFFALDINO: [*announcing to the whole crowd*] This calls for drastic measures. Entertainment number two. You there, bring it out. [*A servant brings out a*

*giant beer keg. Music plays. Perhaps
"Louie, Louie"]*

TRUFFALDINO: Toga! Toga! *[Most of the crowd
begins to crawl and claw all over each
other to get to the keg with the
exception of the royalty and advisors
who laugh heartily at this. Even Leandro
and Clarice cannot help but chuckle. The
prince is still stoic but has succeeded
in freeing himself from his binds by
this point. Most of the people are now
lying in a drunken pile on top of the
keg and Truffaldino has begun to throw
them off one by one. On the bottom of
the pile is Morgana trying to protect
herself from the onslaught. Truffaldino
instantly recognizes her.]* Who let you
in here, you old Wi-atch?

FATA MORGANA: Fool. Mind your own business.
You know you are no match for me.

TRUFFALDINO: You don't belong here. You're up
to no good I know that much.

*[Fata Morgana pushes him. He stands shocked
for a minute then he pushes her back. She
slaps him. He goes to punch her and she ducks,
but when he turns to look at the crowd and
lifts his arms in confusion, he hits her
accidentally. She stomps on his foot. He hops
around in pain. She goes to slap him and
Truffaldino ducks and avoids getting slapped.
Everyone else on stage, however, reacts as if
they were slapped. Morgana, remembering that
she has magic after all, begins to power up
for a big zap. Everyone on stage hides/covers
their eyes to avoid the gruesome scene except
the narrator and Tartaglia. As Morgana gets a
running head start, the narrator trips her and
she falls forward, bouncing off the cowering*

Truffaldino and flips comically over revealing her knickers and striped stockings ala Wizard of Oz. The rest of the crowd looks only in time to see her on the ground and Truffaldino looking down at her and begins applauding and hailing him as the hero. The narrator begins to shush their din and soon the only sound is that of Tartaglia who has been laughing hysterically since she fell over. Everyone in the court begins to celebrate anew with the exception of Leandro, Brighella, and Clarice who begin to sneak off. Smeraldina goes to help a fuming Morgana up.]

KING: My dear Truffaldino, you have saved my son! You get the prize! *[He hands him the large sack of gold. General rejoicing and applause on stage.]*

FATA MORGANA: *[furiously stopping all the rejoicing. Magical flash]* Stop this! Shut up! Silence! Shut up and listen to me. *[Most of the crowd is silenced, though Tartaglia still laughs. Morgana zaps his arms so they are frozen behind him and he begins to listen attentively.]* Listen to me, you braying ass.

> There is one thing they know
> From Berlin to Montana.
> It never is wise
> To cross Fata Morgana. *[chord]*
> Oh of course she's a beauty.
> There is no mistake.
> But she's not nice, like a bunny,
> Has a bite like a snake.
> So laugh it up, sugar!
> But tell all your friends
> That Fata Morgana *[chord]*
> Still got her revenge.
> Enjoying yourself?

Getting caught in my verse?
Well it's more than just poetry.
This is a curse.
You've never known love?
Here's a present from me.
You'll fall in love with an orange
Better yet, make it three!
These three specific oranges
You'll chase 'round the globe
Cause I won't let you stop
Till you wear your death robe.
Nothing else will suffice
From cheese to soda fizz
Because the cause of your death
Will be the love of three oranges!
Run! Run! Find them if you can! *[She laughs triumphantly, then disappears in a poof of smoke.]*

TARTAGLIA: Where are the three oranges? Where are they? My precious oranges! I'm coming! I'm coming my dears! Where? Where? *[He rushes offstage.]*

KING: Tartaglia! Stop! Stop! My son! Stop!

[General confusion on stage. Everyone runs off in different directions. The Narrator is the only one left.]

NARRATOR: Whew! I don't know about the rest of you but I could sure use a smoke. What do you say we meet back here in ten minutes?

ACT II

Act 2, Scene I

[The lights come up on the palace. A good minute passes and nothing happens. Finally the Narrator runs into the theatre, frantically, sits down in a long jacket, whispers "Sorry!" to the audience, and claps to let things begin. Pantalone enters giving instructions to servants who run back and forth getting the Prince things for his trip. He then notices the audience and begins to fill them in.]

PANTALONE: What a change! What a change! So, much has happened! Who would have believed it! Let's recap, shall we? *[For the following, he has cards with each of the characters badly drawn on. He indicates each of them as he goes.]* Prince Tartaglia, who was confined to his room, dying of hypochondria only an Act ago, is now obsessed with leaving the castle, and all because of that witch, Fata Morgana. *[chord]* The clown Truffaldino had finally made him laugh, curing him of her first curse when she suddenly cursed him to fall in love with three specific oranges. Why any old oranges won't do is beyond me. It's not like we don't have hundreds of them in the royal kitchen that he could have his pick of! But, alas, he is determined to go. Nothing can calm the prince or restrain him from this impossible quest. I think this whole thing is beginning to sound like a fairy tale *[a pause]* on crack.

[In marches Tartaglia with great purpose followed meekly by Truffaldino and a servant [or two] who carries a bag. Pantalone hides from Tartaglia's wrath behind the cards and then sneaks out.]

TARTAGLIA: Well, where are they? I've waited for over an hour now. *[Truffaldino opens the shoe bag and takes out a pair of sneakers or whatever shoe you find funniest.]* Keds? I ask you to get me iron shoes that will last me throughout my quest around the world and you hand me Keds? *[He beats Truffaldino with them and then throws them offstage.]*

TRUFFALDINO: But where am I supposed to find a pair of iron shoes?

TARTAGLIA: Did you try a shoe store?

TRUFFALDINO: Yes! I even went to a blacksmith and he thought I was a lunatic.

TARTAGLIA: Well, come up with something. *[Truffaldino shrugs to the servants who walk off in confusion.]* I've got to have them. I've got to get to those wonderful, beautiful, succulent, juicy three oranges. It is bad enough that my father never let me have my own armor and I will have to make it myself, now I have to put up with this idiocy! As soon as I get those shoes, I will embark on my quest for those three tantalizing oranges and you, good sir, will be my squire.

TRUFFALDINO: Now wait just a minute! I didn't mind coming here to save you from the

first curse, but I am the great
Truffaldino, a professional clown, not
your servant.

TARTAGLIA: *[considers this for a moment]* True.
But you must understand that I don't
care. I must save those oranges and make
them mine! *[Servant enters with pieces
for his armor.]* Whatever took you so
long?

*[He begins to take the pieces and tries to
figure out how to wear these pieces.
Eventually he decides on the following: His
helmet is a colander, shoulder pads are small
pots, his legs have cheese graters strapped on
to them and the breast plate is a silver
dinner platter, etc]*

TRUFFALDINO: *[to narrator]* Is he allowed to
pull this?

NARRATOR: Just humor him and keep him safe!

TARTAGLIA: *[requiring some help]* Squire?

TRUFFALDINO: *[with a sigh of exasperation,
going to help him]* Coming, Your Majesty.
*[after some comedy with dressing for
battle]* Your highness, something has
been troubling me. We have no idea where
these oranges are. Where are we going to
be questing to? Wouldn't it be better to
stay at the castle and send scouts. . .

TARTAGLIA: Aha, my good squire, you
underestimate the power of my love and
resolve. I am wiser than you know. They
are two thousand miles away in the
castle of the evil witch, Creonta.

[Confidentially] I overheard the narrator talking during intermission. *[The narrator smacks his forehead.]*

TRUFFALDINO: *[to the narrator]* Thanks a lot, boss.

TARTAGLIA: So we are now ready to begin our quest. Ready, that is, as soon as I get my damn shoes! *[The servants reenter with shoes obviously improvised from household objects like an iron and a pot. The prince is quite pleased by them. Truffaldino thinks they are hysterical but tries to hide it.]* Ah! Wonderful! *[He puts them on and begins to tramp about the stage. The shoes are very heavy and make a good deal of noise.]* Truff, old boy, let's get our bags! We are off! *[Just as they begin to exit, the King, Pantalone, and guards enter.]*

KING: *[More mock tragedy style. Sappy music]* Stay, my son. Stay, I beseech you, for you will surely die on such a long journey. Do not leave the court, I beg you. This is a false love that you feel! It is only the curse of that witch Morgana and this path does not lead to happiness but rather to your death and my despair. I understand how you must feel. I was young once and fancied myself in love. But there are other fish in the sea, other produce in the great supermarket of life. Oh, for all the love that any son ever had for his father, please do not go to your death!

TARTAGLIA: Whatever, Dad. You never understood me anyway. The oranges and I are meant to be together. Get out of my way, for I must rescue them.

KING: How much sharper than a serpent's tooth is an ungrateful child! You give them an inch and they beat you with the yardstick. For God's sake I'm King and I still get no respect.

TARTAGLIA: *[big moment of defiance]* Come, Truffaldino, we must go.

KING: *[dives on the floor and grabs his sons leg]* No. Stay. Stop.

PANTALONE: *[dives on the floor and grabs the other leg]* But we've got so many oranges in this kingdom. Wouldn't three of them do?

TARTAGLIA: I knew you wouldn't understand how I feel. I'm sorry, Father, but my destiny calls me! Farewell!

[Tartaglia tires to leave but they have him too tightly. He snaps for Truffaldino who tries to pry them off and eventually decides to lift him out of it. The King faints. Truffaldino carries the prince off. The prince blows a kiss on the way out. The king jumps up to see this and then faints again. Pantalone fans him. Princess Clarice, Leandro, and Brighella hurry on to the stage.]

CLARICE: *[to Pantalone]* What was all that racket? Some of us are trying to make evil plans *[they all throw her a glance]*. . . I mean sleep.

LEANDRO: What is everyone doing?

PANTALONE: Well, the Prince and Truffaldino have just gone to find the oranges, the King has just fainted, I'm fanning him, you want to know what everyone is doing, and *[meaning the audience]* they're just kind of sitting there watching it all!

BRIGHELLA: DAH! You are making my brain hurt! I feel like I'm in a Stoppard play!

KING: *[recovering, then raving in a tragic manner.]* Oh, alas is me! Alas! My son! My precious son! My son is as good as dead! We may as well just end the play now! Everyone just go home! Evil has won! *[Evil trio celebrates behind his back. When he turns to them on the next line, they feign sorrow.]* The whole court must dress in black. I will end my days in weeping and loneliness. Alas. Alas.

PANTALONE: Oh, my King. I will weep with you. We will shed our tears together into one handkerchief   -   then   give   that handkerchief to some poet to inspire him.

KING: Oh, shut up, Pantalone.

[The King exits, followed by Pantalone and the guards. The evil trio applaud themselves and slap hands all around.]

BRIGHELLA: Booyah!

CLARICE: Hooray for Morgana! The kingdom is as good as ours!

LEANDRO: Indeed. Well, we'd better come to some understanding about rights and the divisions of powers. I, of course, will have the bulk of the power. . .

CLARICE: *[very intense, rubbing hands together]* I want to be the general of the armies and wage wars! *[They look at her with mild concern. She catches herself and says flightily]* Oh, did I say armies? I meant puppies! *[they accept this with a slightly suspicious look]*

BRIGHELLA: Well, since I've been such a loyal lackey, I want a position too. All I want is to be in charge of the court's entertainments. I want to be the master of revels, the raja of rubber chickens, the workman of the whoopee cushion! *[Leandro and Clarice gag and look ill]*

LEANDRO: Comedies! Spare us! Please don't assault the gentle. sensibilities of the theatre going public by brandishing about bodily functions and the ribald! It cannot possibly be considered art unless your work forces the audience to sit back and ponder the human condition or at least shed a tear. With times as they are, we need to examine why we, as a people, have become so worthless and why we even bother to go on.

BRIGHELLA: *[Reluctant]* I don't know. I bet a lot of people would like to laugh and forget about. . .

CLARICE: You are so stupid. You don't understand anything.

LEANDRO: If you had your way, you would likely have us revive those idiotic commedia plays and have us all reading children's stories again. *[laughs]*

CLARICE: *[laughs]* With a fairy tale story and simple, obvious villains that the heroes give their comeuppance in the end!

LEANDRO: How completely inapplicable to the modern world. No one is interested in seeing good vs. evil. You are such a fool!

[They both exit, laughing. Brighella looks around the empty stage. To audience.]

BRIGHELLA: I kinda like them. *[He exits.]*

Act 2, Scene 2

X2C From L

[*The narrator turns the page as he speaks. The scene changes to an ominous wilderness and caldron. There are no actors on stage, save the narrator.*]

NARRATOR: A large, ominous wilderness. Celio, the good magician, nemesis to Fata Morgana, and the protector of Prince Tartaglia, was making circles on the ground to summon the devil Farfarello to his aid. For Celio, you see, was more powerful than Morgana knew. He was, in fact, guiding the entire tale along in ways she could never have realized.

ENL

[*He turns as if to clap and let the scene begin, but there is no one there. He seems to panic a little. He gestures to the audience to wait a second and runs off. The stage is empty. The Mute Bumpkin enters from stage right and walks silently with his eyes ahead across the stage. When he reaches center, he turns his head slowly giving a blank faced take to the audience. He then slowly turns his head back to forward and walks the rest of the way offstage. Narrator returns a moment later dressed as a wizard. Some of his costume could be under the jacket. He is Celio. He begins to dramatically draw circles on the ground with his staff. He pauses a moment, just before beginning the scene, to smile at the audience and say:*]

EL (slow dd)(break on line)

CELIO: Oh, please! Like you didn't know it was me all along. [*chanting very seriously as Celio*]

(Big)   Farfarello! Farfarello!

> I order you here.
>
> I now need your service.
>
> Farfarello! Appear!

[aside to the audience] Yeah so spells around here usually rhyme, in case you haven't noticed. If you have a problem with that convention, I'll see you after the curtain call. *[he casts the final ingredient in. Big puff of smoke and a flash.]*

FARFARELLO: *[appears but does not yet have sight. In a large imposing voice]* Who calls me? Who orders me from the bowels of the earth?

CELIO: It is I, Celio.

FARFARELLO: Who? *[sees him for the first time. Drops big voice. A little effeminate.]* O jeez! Are we in a play? Or, don't even tell me, you're just a stage magician! Do you have any idea how tired I am of having to play the lovely assistant? If you're only from some silly old play, I will march right back down to the bowels of the earth.

CELIO: I am a real magician. Stay! I order you!

FARFARELLO: Are you sure this isn't a big act? I could swear that's stage makeup on your face. Though this place is awfully pathetic for a Vegas show room. *[to the audience]* They didn't even feed you, huh? And don't even get me started with that outfit? Honestly, tell me you put that on this morning and said "I look good."

CELIO: *[He shakes his staff and there is lighting and thunder]* Enough of this impertinence. I sent Truffaldino to the King of Heart's court to help Prince Tartaglia to laugh and be cured of his terminal hypochondria. Where are they now?

FARFARELLO: *[impressed]* Ooo! That's nice. That was a good voice. It sounded very authentic. I think I got chills! *[Celio makes like he is going to zap him. This intimidates him.]* OK, I'll tell you what. Union doesn't want us wasting the powers of the occult on stupid performances but you seem authentic enough so I'll obey you.

CELIO: *[heavily sarcastic]* How big of you.

FARFARELLO: Truffaldino is still with the Prince, trying to help him but Morgana has summoned a wind god to speed them towards their destination, so sure is she that Creonta and the perils of her castle will destroy them for good. *[very eager]* So let me guess? You summoned me to help, right? You're Mr. All Powerful with the lightning and all but you can't be in two places at once so you want me to stop the wind god, right?

CELIO: *[still sarcastic]* No, I was hoping you'd give me a nice full body massage.

FARFARELLO: *[interested]* Really? OH, yeah now that you mention it, you do look tight. Because let me tell you, I have magic everywhere and these hands are positively enchanting. . . *[Look from Celio. Stops himself]* Oh, you were kidding. Should have figured as much. Not like anyone ever calls me out of hell just to say hi or for a cup of coffee. The devil doesn't allow conjugal visits you know . . .*[Celio readies himself to* zap *again]* OK, look. I can. . . *[clears throat and goes back to big voice. Formal]* I can distract the wind god and lead him away from your charges and give you this *[he presents a sack]* to help them through the perils but to be quite frank, I'm not much more help.

CELIO: *[formal]* Thank you, Farfarello.

FARFARELLO: *[bows. Drops big voice.]* Well, it's been real, but I have to go back to the bowels of the earth now. Bye! *[he disappears]*

CELIO: *[dramatic music]* Even with this help, their path will be dangerous. I must try to dissuade them from this desperate task or at the very least help them to find these three oranges and thus break Morgana's spell. I only hope these tools from the underworld will be enough to save them from the hideous and inhuman perils that await them yet.

[Yet more big dramatic music, flourish, and Celio exits.]

Act 2, Scene 3

[The forest near Creonta's Castle. Strike the caldron. It's a different part of the forest. Change the lights if you want. Move a log. Go nuts. Truffaldino and Tartaglia enter being blown by the Wind God with two paper fans. They are struggling to fight against the wind but it blows them further along. They run very fast but after a few laps around the stage Farfarello appears and whistles to get the Wind God's attention. He lures him off with a pinwheel. They both fall once the pressure of the wind is gone.]

TRUFFALDINO: Oh! What the heck was that all about?

TARTAGLIA: What time we've made! I can almost smell those wonderful oranges. Ah, there it is! The castle of Creonta.

TRUFFALDINO: O wonderful. Well, let's camp here and check it out tomorrow. I'm tired and hungry. Let's find something to eat and then take a little nap. . .

TARTAGLIA: How can you be concerned with food now when the castle is there in the distance? We must storm the castle of Creonta! We must rescue those three oranges for I love them. We must...

[Thunderclap. Celio appears.]

CELIO: Stop, hasty prince. The Castle of Creonta is fraught with dangers for you and your servant. You would be lucky to get out alive. *[scary intimidating music*

begins] There are horrors untold that guard the place. There is an ancient iron gate rusted by time, *[they gasp]* an ornery donkey, *[Truffaldino screams and runs behind a tree]* an old evil rope, and an ugly old hag of a cook who does not have a broom and must sweep out her oven with her own sagging breasts.

TARTAGLIA: Riiiiiight. *[music switches to triumphant]* Don't try to scare me with those horror stories. I am determined to try to save those three wonderful oranges that I love. Love has no fear. Those oranges will bring me happiness and you cannot keep me from them. *[music swells and then stops]*

CELIO: Well, young prince, since you are so determined to get to those three oranges, here are some powerful tools that should help you. *[gives him the sack]* If you should survive these unspeakable horrors and get to the three oranges, take them and leave the castle at once. But remember, and this is the most important thing of all, **do not open the oranges unless you are near water**. If you can do all this, I will put a spell on your path that ensures you will have a safe and speedy journey home. Be careful, my young prince.

TARTAGLIA: Thank you, good sir.

[Celio disappears.]

TARTAGLIA: Let us go now. *[Truffaldino terrified and is not moving an inch]* Good heavens, man! We are heroes! And heroes must be brave no matter what the odds. What of all the damsels in need of rescuing?

TRUFFALDINO: *[terrified]* Oh, I'm all about rescuing damsels. I'm just not that willing to risk my life for a few pieces of citrus is all. What's the big hurry? This donkey and witch and whole venture is beginning to sound very dangerous to me. *[Sits on a log]*

TARTAGLIA: *[Sits next to him. Earnest.]* Truff. I need you. You are the only real friend I've ever had. *[Puts his hand on Truffaldino's leg. Truffaldino looks at him. Perhaps play the opening of the theme from Cheers. An uncomfortable moment. They jump up and go to opposite sides of the stage]*

TRUFFALDINO: Oh, now you've gone and made me feel all guilty. Why don't I just stay and watch the camp? You could just scout ahead. . . *[Tartaglia has already started off. Truffaldino sighs and begins to walk begrudgingly off.]* Right. Following.

Act 2, Scene 4

[In Fata Morgana's castle]

NARRATOR: *[crossing the stage and turning the page]* Meanwhile, in the castle of Fata Morgana. . .

BRIGHELLA: You've been quiet.

SMERALDINA: I had no lines!

BRIGHELLA: For an entire act and then some?

SMERALDINA: Listen, buddy. Quite or not, I'm 8 million times the henchman that you are. I am the most evil damn lackey that ever was. All that silence? *[taps her head]* Evil plotting!

BRIGHELLA: Oh yeah! Well I'm so evil I post spoilers for TV shows on the Internet.

SMERALDINA: *[toying with him]* Really? I'm so evil I once sprayed my hair with an aerosol can, even when I didn't need that tight hold, just to mess with the ozone layer.

BRIGHELLA: I'm so evil, I don't always wash my hands after leaving the rest room.

SMERALDINA: Well, I'm so evil I know how many licks it takes to get to the center of a tootsie pop, but I won't tell.

BRIGHELLA: Sweet Satan you are evil!

SMERALDINA: Punish me! *[they throw everything off a nearby table and jump on it, beginning to kiss and tear clothing off when Morgana arrives. Brighella shrieks upon seeing her, falls off the table, tries to hide under it, climbs all the way through to the other side. Sees Morgana and shrieks again and then jumps on onto the table and sits next to Smeraldina [still laying down] and tries to play it cool. Smeraldina is amused. Morgana is disgusted.]*

BRIGHELLA: Yes. . .So. . .I think they're probably dead by now.

SMERALDINA: Yeah. Dead. Definitely.

FATA MORGANA: OK. Ew. All right. Shut up, you two. We've got trouble. That infernal wizard Celio is helping Tartaglia and Truffaldino, who unfortunately for the both of you are very much not dead. I don't understand. Celio has some way to have control over everyone's actions but I cannot figure out how. We must discover it and beat him at his own game. Both of you, follow me! If Creonta doesn't kill them, we'll need to have something else up our sleeve. *[the sidekicks exit. Morgana stops to throw a final line at the audience]* He'll rue the day he messed with Fata Morgana! *[Chord. Exit.]*

Act 2, Scene 5

[A courtyard in the witch Creonta's castle.]

NARRATOR: *[crossing the stage, turning the page]* All too soon, our heroes reached the courtyard of Queen Creonta's castle.

[A big flourish of dramatic music accompanies each of the "horrors". Prince Tartaglia and Truffaldino come up to the gate with great fear [it may growl at them and then quietly whisper "Oil Can"] and then reach into the bag and find oil, which Tartaglia tentatively puts on and the gate slowly swings open so they can enter. They get through the gate and the donkey runs out and begins to bray at them menacingly, but Prince Tartaglia reaches into the bag and throws him some carrots, which he happily eats. The lights reveal the coiled rope, the most terrifying thing of all. Truffaldino, obviously very afraid, helps the prince to uncoil the rope and they stretch it out to dry. The cook enters quickly.]

THE COOK: Who's there? I'll kill you, I will! There is no trespassing on Queen Creonta's property. And keep it down or you'll ruin the soufflé I have in there.

TRUFFALDINO: Dear Madame, we have brought a gift for you. *[He grandly gives her a dust buster from the bag while Tartaglia sneaks into the castle.]*

THE COOK: A dust buster! *[revs it up once]* You sweet little thing! I don't have to use my poor old breasts to clean out that oven anymore! Oh, thank you!

[She hugs him. The cook fancies Truffaldino and begins to flirt with him. During this Prince Tartaglia has gone into the castle and comes out pulling a wagon with three huge, magic oranges on it. For the sake of simplicity, the Oranges can also tiptoe along single file, tied together at the waist. Then a horrible figure appears in the upper tower of the castle. Unlike Morgana, Creonta is a hideous hag.]

CREONTA: Stop, thief! Those oranges are mine. Drop them immediately! *[Tartaglia is momentarily intimidated and then blows her a raspberry and continues. She makes a sound of frustration and screams.]* You, cook, grab those two and throw them into your oven immediately!

THE COOK: No, sugar, I really don't think I will. I've been cleaning that damned oven of yours year after year. You've just sat there, day after day and watched my cup size go up and never gave me so much as a broom, but those two nice young men did. These handsome fellows have shown me the light. I'm not going to obey you anymore.

[She gives Truffaldino a farewell kiss and a tray of muffins. Though Truffaldino was unsure of her at first, this wins him over. The prince has to pull him away. He and the prince begin to leave the courtyard when Creonta appears at a different window.]

CREONTA: Rope, you rope! Hang those two thieves by the neck until they are dead.

THE ROPE: Alack, but vile and ill-natured female! Upon wherein did thine affections tarry when I didst but lie here and rot for many a year? Nay, but those fellows tooketh care to remove the wetness that didst plagueth me of late and hath laid me upon the cool ground to revel in a state of dryness. Nay, I wouldst not delay them in their noble course for all thine base and bestial howling.

CREONTA: Then, you, dearest donkey, precious beast of burden, tear those two apart and eat their flesh!

DONKEY: Nay, but alas for many a season didst you but keep the food of the tummy from me and my mouth when it was that I required it of you. These fine gentlemen of fortune didst but give me carrots of which to partake which I did most verily and forthsoothe with merriment. I havest decided that thou dost suck most verily and no longer will I layth the smackth down in thine name but will rather let such gentlemen as these go free of themselves.

TRUFFALDINO: *[To the audience.]* Well, what do you know? Fakespeare! *[the musician musically emphasizes the lameness of this joke. The heroes are almost out of the courtyard. Creonta suddenly appears behind them. They begin to run towards the gate.]*

CREONTA: You, gate! Lock immediately. Keep them here in my courtyard and I'll catch them myself and eat them alive.

THE GATE: No way in hell, witch! Where's the love? Did you ever oil me? Hell no. You

just let my ass rust off out here year
after year, so there ain't no way in
hell I'd lock my dawgs in here, who gave
me some sweet sweet oil. God speed
gentlemen. *[Prince Tartaglia and
Truffaldino stand amazed at hearing
this.]*

TARTAGLIA: Oh, gate, donkey, rope, cook! Thank
you. Thank you very much. *[Tartaglia and
Truffaldino quickly exit with the three
oranges.]*

CREONTA: You miserable gate! You stupid
donkey, you. Where is that bitch of a
cook? And you, you miserable excuse for
a rope! He's taken them! My oranges! My
precious oranges! *[She roars.]* Oh, God!
God! God, how could you have allowed
this? How could you let this happen to
me? You know what, God? You suck. I bet
you don't even exist! OO! Look at me!
Dancing on the edge of the smite zone!
If you do exist, God, I dare you to
strike me dead right here, right now!

*[A thunderbolt. She is struck dead. Celio, who
snuck in and saw the end of this watches this
with glee and begins to turn the page with a
laugh and then run off the stage. Unbeknownst
to him, Fata Morgana spies this and, curious,
follows him offstage. Which is why she is not
there to meet Smeraldina at the start of Act
III.]*

ACT III

Act 3, Scene I

[The scene changes to another part of the forest with some rocks or a log high enough for Smeraldina to sit on. Smeraldina alone, waiting.]

SMERALDINA: Where is she? Is this the right place? *[takes out a cell phone and checks. Reads in monotone.]* "Smeraldina, meet me by the big log so that I can tell you your pivotal role in my brilliant evil plan. LOL. Ttyl." Nope this is the place. Finally my chance to be in the spotlight! All this time waiting in the wings, quietly watching everyone else's chance to steal the scene and finally I get a chance to nibble on some of the scenery. Just when I was starting to feel like my only function was a pathetic attempt to balance out the gender ratio. Pivotal role! I will show that powerless, self absorbed, cauldron licking . . . *[Fata Morgana enters. Smeraldina catches herself.]*

FATA MORGANA: Well, there is nothing but bad news from Hell.

SMERALDINA: What kind of news were you expecting from Hell?

FATA MORGANA: Don't get sassy on me! As I said, bad news from Hell. Creonta has failed us. That vile Celio has helped Prince Tartaglia and Truffaldino to get the oranges. We must take care of the meddling wizard once and for all. And I

think I finally figured out how. This
plan cannot fail!

SMERALDINA: Right, just like making him a
hypochondriac killed him right away. Oh,
wait! That plan actually failed, didn't
it? Then the quest for the oranges was
going to kill him and then Creonta. I
thought you were supposed to be an all
powerful mistress of the dark arts? I
thought you said we could not fail?

FATA MORGANA: Shut up! Shut up! Shut up! Bad
days happen to even Fata Morgana.
[Chord. It reassures her.] So, shut up!

SMERALDINA: *[under her breath]* Some sinister
villainess you are.

FATA MORGANA: I would kill you this instant,
you disrespectful wench, if I did not
need you for the final stage of the
plan. Truffaldino and the prince will be
here soon and then we will teach Celio a
lesson and finish him off once and for
all. Your job is simple, Smeraldina.
When the princess . . .

SMERALDINA: Wait a second. Did I miss
something? What princess? There is no
princess in this story!

FATA MORGANA: Do you honestly believe we would
have a story with a wizard and princes
and kings and witches but no princess?
You are as foolish as I always believed.
No wonder you've always sat on the
sidelines. You aren't smart enough to do
anything yourself. *[Smeraldina fumes but
says nothing.]* When the princess, and
there will be one, is left alone, you

will gain her confidence and then put this bobby pin in her hair.

SMERALDINA: What? That's my pivotal role? To make sure some princess's hair isn't mussed? I get to play hairdresser to some character who only waltzes in on Act III? I quit. *[Starts to leave]*

FATA MORGANA: Fool! It will make her transform into a dove! *[music]* Once she has transformed, you will then sit in her place. *[little more music]* Prince Tartaglia will be forced to marry you and make you his queen. *[still more music]* Then, once you are Queen, put this other pin in his head and he, too, will become a beast. *[even more music]* Then you will leave the castle and let Princess Clarice and Leandro rule the kingdom. *[small concluding flourish]* Understand?

SMERALDINA: Wait a minute. So let me get this straight. I get rid of the real princess, *[music]* marry the Prince, *[little more music]* become Queen *[still more music]* and then just leave and go back to being a lackey while Clarice and Leandro, who have been sitting on their laurels this whole time, plotting but never actually doing anything, get to rule the kingdom? How is that even remotely fair? Why can't I just stay the queen?

FATA MORGANA: I have a whole bag of these, Smeraldina! *[shows a bag of bobby pins. Biggest most exaggerated dramatic music of all. To the heavens]* Ok, now that was just excessive!

MUSICIAN: Sorry!

SMERALDINA: But. . .

FATA MORGANA: Sh . . . Sh . . . I hear
     somebody. Come with me.

*[They exit. Two bumpkins walk onto the stage.
The Mute Bumpkin holds a sign that says "LAKE
OF MUCH WATER" in large letters and an arrow
pointing just offstage. In the meantime,
Truffaldino enters pulling the wagon on which
there are the three large oranges but doesn't
notice the bumpkins over his own panting. The
muffin tray is empty now.]*

BUMPKIN 1: This looks like as good a place as
     any for this. Did you bring the hammer?
     [Mute Bumpkin shakes his head] Oh, I
     thought you had it. Just stay here. I'll
     be right back with it. *[Mute Bumpkin
     stays, holding the sign, waiting and
     watching the proceedings.]*

TRUFFALDINO: *[out of breath]* I miss that guy
     with the fans! At least now the castle
     is in sight. *[to audience]* Oh, hello!
     You're not going to believe this, but
     guess who is suddenly wondering what the
     heck we are going to do with these three
     huge oranges now that we've 'rescued'
     them.

VOICE: The playwright?

TRUFFALDINO: No, not the playwright. It's our
     favorite monarch back there, Prince
     Tartaglia. No sooner did we leave
     Creonta's castle then the curse started
     to wear off. And as soon as it began to

wear off, Tartaglia began to realize what the rest of us have seen all along. That, after all this work, all we have to show for it is these three silly giant oranges. He's been lagging behind the last few miles, lost in thought. *[sniffs. The smell of oranges begins to fill the theatre]* What is that? Are there Soccer Moms around here somewhere? *[loud sound of his stomach growling]* Oh, no! The problem with standing still is that now I'm starting to notice how hungry I am. OH, how I wish I had something to eat. Just something small like a bagel, a muffin, a piece of fruit. . .*[notices the oranges. Gets the idea]* Hmm. No. No, I mustn't. But he does have three of them. What does he need with three of them? Maybe if I just eat one. He may not even remember how many we had to begin with. Two is a nice even number. There is nothing here to tip him off that there were three oranges. *[He is about to cut one of them but pauses and says to the audience]* You better hide your programs, just in case. *[He cuts open one of the oranges. Out of it comes a lovely young girl.]*

NICOLETTA: The sun! It has been so long since I have seen its gentle rays. Oh they are so bright and hot! They are too hot! Oh, I'm so thirsty! Please give me some water! I am so parched! Please, or I'll die of thirst. Oh, I'm so thirsty. Quick, don't be so cruel. Oh, help me... help me... *[She collapses and is dying.]*

TRUFFALDINO: Dah! Where can I find some water? Where could there possibly be water around here?

[He doesn't notice the bumpkin with the sign. The bumpkin begins to subtly point it out]

NICOLETTA: Help me, please... help me...

TRUFFALDINO: Hold on lady. I'll open another orange and get you some of the orange juice to drink. That'll fix you right up.

[He cuts open another orange, out of which comes LINETTA. Truffaldino screams and faints at seeing this.]

LINETTA: I'm finally free! I've been trapped for so long. All those years waiting and finally we have been rescued. I would like a drink, though. Oh the cruel sun! Oh, I'm dying of thirst. Please, please, give me something to drink. I'm dying of thirst. Oh, please help me! Cruel man, help me... help me ...

TRUFFALDINO: *[jumping back up]* If only I had some indication or sign where I could find water! Where is there water? Oh! Oh! What can I do? What can I do? Where can I find some water? Where?

NICOLETTA: Oh, what a fate. I'm dying of thirst! I'm dying... *[She dies.]*

LINETTA: I'm dying, you cruel man. Oh, oh! Help me... help me... help me... *[She dies.]*

TRUFFALDINO: Oh! Oh! Maybe if I open the third orange I can use the juice from that to save these two?

[As he is about to cut open the third orange, Prince Tartaglia enters quickly and sees what happened.]

TARTAGLIA: *[Sees the oranges]* Truffaldino! Stop! What are you doing? The wizard said that we've got to be near water before we open them. Stop! *[Truffaldino runs off. Tartaglia begins a dramatic mourning for the girls. Music becomes highly tragic. Mute Bumpkin hangs his head in sadness and maybe crosses himself or blows his nose.]* Truffaldino, you fool. What's this? Oh no! These poor young girls. Dead? Dead? They were but in the spring of their life and now that life has been plucked off them as feathers off a roasted chicken. Alas! How short is our time upon this earth! *[The prince suddenly calls off stage.]* Hey! Hey, you! Can we get some clean-up out here? *[Two country bumpkins enter.]* Yeah just get rid of these two won't you? They're bringing the whole scene down.

BUMPKIN 2: Sure thing, boss. Our pleasure. What a shame! These poor girls. *[starts to pick them up]*

TARTAGLIA: Thank you for all your help. Can I give you something for your trouble? *[takes out his coin pouch]*

BUMPKIN 3: Oh, sir we could not possibly take your money. But we could use a new coin pouch.

TARTAGLIA: But if I give you my coin pouch, what will I keep my coins in?

BUMPKIN 3: Well, then we are very glad that we can help you in that area too, sir. We will take those too. *[Takes coin purse. Prince Tartaglia is very thankful.]*

BUMPKIN 2: You're a real Prince. Don't worry, we'll give these girls a decent burial.

[The two bumpkins drag the two girls unceremoniously offstage. It is only after they leave that the Prince realizes he has been swindled]

TARTAGLIA: Hey! Wait! *[they are gone]* And now I only have one orange left. How big and beautiful it orange is! How lovely and tender is its skin. How delicious! I must cut it open and just take a tiny peek at what it holds.

[Mute Bumpkin runs up as if to stop him but doesn't make it in time. He takes out his sword and opens the last one. Out pops Ninetta.]

NINETTA: Who took me out of my orange? Oh! The cruel sun! I am so parched! Help me! Help me! Please! Please! Bring me some water! *[She collapses.]*

TARTAGLIA: Oh yeah! Water? I apparently have no short term memory. I forgot! Where can I possibly find water around here? *[he begins to spaz idiotically as Truffaldino did but is stopped as the Mute Bumpkin smacks him with the sign and points to it]* Ah thank you my good man!

*[The Prince runs offstage. The Bumpkin and the
dying Ninetta look at each other. He gives her
a little wave. She gives him a weak wave back.
He smiles at her and exits as Tartaglia runs
back on, with one of his iron shoes filled
with water*

TARTAGLIA: Excuse the vessel, dear lady, but
here's some water.

*[She drinks the water, her face buried in the
shoe. She slowly lowers the shoe after her
drink and Tartaglia really sees her for the
first time. It is instant love. Sappy music to
indicate as such.]*

NINETTA: Oh, thank you, most heroic sir. You
have saved my life.

TARTAGLIA: Are you OK?

NINETTA: *[meaning her love]* I don't think I'll
ever be the same. *[catches herself]* I
mean to say, I've been in an orange.

TARTAGLIA: Please, my dearest lady, let me
help you. My goodness! So, tell me. What
was a girl like you doing in an orange
like this?

NINETTA: Well, I wasn't always an orange. I am
actually a princess and Ninetta is my
name. I am the daughter of Concul, King
of Antipodes, but I and my two beloved
sisters were turned into oranges by the
wicked witch Creonta. I know it all
sounds so improbable, but believe me, it
really happened.

TARTAGLIA: Oh, after everything else that has gone on today, I have no difficulty believing your story, Princess.

NINETTA: Oh my dearest sisters! How I love them! I do hope they are happy and well. Have you seen them, fair sir?

TARTAGLIA: *[guiltily]* Uh. . no. I just got here myself. I'm sure they are fine. Oh, but Princess Ninetta! You have other things to think about. For I am Prince Tartaglia, my father is the King of Hearts, and you are the most amazing creature I have ever seen. I have never known such complete happiness in all my life as you make me feel. Ninetta, I believe I am in love with you. Will you make me this happy forever? Will you marry me and be my Queen of Hearts, since you already rule over mine?

NINETTA: We just met three seconds ago! Isn't this a bit sudden? People certainly do fall in love fast in this story! Though, you are fairly handsome, and it's so nice to be a princess again instead of an orange. Oh, OK sure! *[He dips her over and they kiss. While mid-kiss Ninetta turns to the audience and says]* Oh, give me a break. You spend a few years in an orange and see how picky you are! *[returns to the kiss. to him]* I feel like we're in a fairy tale.

Reek on kiss

TARTAGLIA: We are, my jewel, which means we are guaranteed the happily ever after. I cannot wait to present you to my father.

NINETTA: Oh, but this dress is covered in pulp. I have nothing suitable to meet a king in.

TARTAGLIA: My precious, my father will love you no matter how you are dressed, but if you insist, I'll bring the whole court to you along with some fine clothes fit for a princess. Wait here my love while I go tell my father about the beautiful creature I promised to marry.

NINETTA: My love! My dear water boy! I will wait for you.

TARTAGLIA: *[steals many pecks throughout this exchange]* Yes, yes, my future queen. Wait for me here.

NINETTA: I promise to stay right here.

TARTAGLIA: And I promise to hurry back and marry you.

[He exits. The narrator, who has been watching the last bit from the house freezes Ninetta with a clap and then walks onto the stage. He smiles, has a contented sigh and then tries to end the play. Morgana spies on this from behind.] Enter Left ✗ᴸ

CELIO: And so it was that the Prince returned to the Kingdom with a new bride. They married and the Prince finally had someone who could truly touch his heart. So the King and Queen ruled their kingdom with kindness and laughter and everyone lived happily ever. . .

FATA MORGANA: *[bursting on stage]* Not so fast, Celio! *[she freezes him with a snap]*

> You ruined my revenge
>
> But I've planned for all these hours
>
> And now with one simple spell
>
> I negate all your powers!
>
> You've been running this show.
>
> Every choice was your choice.
>
> Well I'd like to see you narrate
>
> If you don't have a voice!

[Morgana unfreezes him and bursts into evil laughter. Celio tries to continue with his narration but no sound comes out of his mouth. He tries silently shouting at Morgana but she only laughs at him.]

FATA MORGANA: Oh, try all you wish, Celio. You cannot stop me now! You are powerless. You are one of the characters in the story just like everyone else now. Brighella! Smeraldina! *[Brighella and Smeraldina enter hurriedly putting their clothing back on]* Grab him! *[the lackeys grab him and drag him kicking and silently screaming offstage]* It's about time we had a fairy tale where evil put up a decent fight. *[to the audience]* Sorry for the inconvenience, everyone, but I'm telling this story now! And I'm going to make sure that it turns out my way! Miserably ever after for Silvio and Tartaglia. *[Morgana goes gleefully to sit in the audience. She unfreezes Ninetta]* Smeraldina! You're on!

SMERALDINA: Whoa, honey! You are having one hell of a bad hair day!

NINETTA: Am I? O dear! Can you help me fix it? There are no mirrors in this forest and I've been in a very awkward position in an orange for a long time.

SMERALDINA: You don't say?

NINETTA: Yes, it was a rather large orange and it mussed my hair.

SMERALDINA: Here, let me fix it for you.

[She puts the bobby pin in her head; Ninetta turns into a dove and flies off. This is easiest accomplished by the actress carrying a dove puppet and the other characters simply only watching the puppet and ignoring her. She coos. Smeraldina tries to catch it to no avail]

SMERALDINA: *[shouts out to Morgana]* Hey boss? I didn't get to kill her. She left too fast. You want me to go after her?

FATA MORGANA: No need, Smeraldina. I am running this story now. In fact, I am tired of waiting. What do you say Prince Tartaglia comes back right now. *[Smeraldina sits on the log and assumes a royal air. Sounds of a royal march are heard offstage. The King of Hearts* *enters, with Prince Tartaglia, Leandro, Princess Clarice, Pantalone, and the court. Narrating.]* The Prince returned with his father and all the court to meet his bride. *[gleeful pause]* And then he walked into a tree. *[he does so]* Twice. *[he does so again. she laughs with great amusement. Tartaglia recovers himself and begins]*

TARTAGLIA: Here she is, father. Here is the princess that I love and want to make my queen. *[he looks at her for the first time]* GAH! Who in the name of Gozzi are you?

SMERALDINA: I am Princess Ninetta, the girl you promised to marry.

TARTAGLIA: You so are not! You are hideous and you have a personality that rivals spore mold. I've had better looking zits. No way in hell will I marry you.

SMERALDINA: That's not what you said last night! *[The crowd reacts with shock]* I never should have trusted you! *[to the King]* He told me he loved me and he promised he would marry me or I never would have... *[she degenerates into exaggerated sobs. Everyone turns accusingly to Tartaglia]*

KING: My son, a royal promise is a royal promise. You must keep your word. You should not make promises in the heat of the moment that you do not intend to keep in the morning light.

TARTAGLIA: Oh, wait! Ew! You people think that I . . . and her. . .? No! I would never even touch. . . *[Smeraldina weeps louder on the shoulder of a servant. She gives Clarice and Leandro a thumbs up over the servant's shoulder.]*

KING: You will marry this princess. I order you to do so!

PANTALONE: But your majesty. . .

KING: No son of mine will go back on his promise. Let us all go back to the palace. This matter is closed. The wedding will be tonight.

[The band strikes up the royal march; all march offstage. Ninetta flies back onstage in time to observe Smeraldina laughing and giving Tartaglia a kiss on the check and a smack on the backside on the way out. Ninetta, filled with jealousy at this, begins to peck Smeraldina on the head as she exits. Tartaglia tries to escape but the royal guards stop him. He reluctantly walks and sobs on the way offstage.]

Act 3, Scene 2

[The stage is cleared. Morgana goes down to center stage to end the play.]

FATA MORGANA: *[enjoying herself immensely]* And so it was that the Prince was forced to marry the woman he found in the forest. That night she put a magic bobby pin in his hair and he turned into a pig whose feet they used for jelly. And the King, at seeing his limping leg-less pig of a son, gouged out his eyes with a broach. So they lived the rest of their days miserably ever. . .

CELIO: *[bursting forward with triumphant music]* Not likely!

FATA MORGANA: What? Where did you come from? How did you get here?

CELIO: I escaped. . . *[wink to the audience]* somehow.

FATA MORGANA: That is impossible! How did you escape? How did you get your voice back? This makes no sense.

CELIO: It doesn't have to. *[Unbeknownst to Celio, Brighella is sneaking up behind him to hit him with a weapon]* See, I know a few things about fairy tales, Morgana, that you seemed to have overlooked. Number 1: Willful suspension of disbelief. Nothing ever has to make sense as long as the audience is amused. Number 2: Things always look bleaker before they get better. But most of all, Number 3: Good always wins, no mater how unlikely or unrealistic it may seem. *[Just as Brighella is about to kill him a ninja-type cry is heard from off stage and Truffaldino appears and hits Brighella with a rubber chicken. Brighella falls over, Celio tosses Truffaldino a cookie, which he catches in his mouth, eats and then drags Brighella offstage]*

FATA MORGANA: Fool! Do you know who you are dealing with? I am Fata Morgana. *[instead of the usual note, out comes a loud "moo"]* What was that?

MUSICIAN: I think it was a cow.

FATA MORGANA: Shut up you fool!

CELIO: You could save yourself a good deal of time, you know, by just walking out right now since we all pretty much know how this is going to end.

FATA MORGANA: You are just trying to make me give up! Never! I challenge you to a duel to the death.

CELIO: *[smiles calmly]* Bring it on.

[They square off. Celio begins to swing his stick around ninja style. Morgana stops his stick mid twirl with magic, raises it up, and twirls him. She then makes him thrust the stick between his legs and laughs as he gasps in pain and throws his stick offstage. He then gains power over her hands and forces her to open her mouth and say "I love Celio. He is

great." *She breaks out of this and turns him into a baby. He begins to crawl around the stage and mistakes Morgana for his Mommy. She flattens him for this error. He gets up and fires a blast at her. She ducks. There is a blast of confetti behind her and Truffaldino comes running out fanning his behind. Morgana fires at Celio. She too misses and there is another blast and Brighella comes running out in the same fashion. Both wizard and witch fire at each other at the same time and the blast ricochets around the room finally hitting Truffaldino and Brighella. They turn into chickens and run offstage. Morgana inflates Celio and he runs around as he is being deflated. As she begins to work the crowd, Celio, tired of this battle, grabs a bookmark from the book and hits her on the head and knocks her unconscious. Truffaldino comes in to congratulate him and Celio drags Morgana off.]* exit.

TRUFFALDINO: OK, everyone let's finish this up so we can all go home! So, Prince Tartaglia is getting married and the King has ordered me to help prepare the wedding feast. But the poor prince is still not happy and won't even talk to his bride. Eh, he's probably better off. That is how most marriages end up anyway. But right now my job is to roast the chicken.

[Truffaldino starts roasting a rubber chicken on a spit. Suddenly a dove appears.]

DOVE: Good day, Mr. Cook.

TRUFFALDINO: Well, howdee, little pretty birdie.

DOVE: I would love for you to fall asleep and burn the chicken so that ugly hag, Smeraldina, does not get to eat any of it.

TRUFFALDINO: Glad to be of service, miss.

[Truffaldino falls asleep on his feet. The rubber chicken burns. The dove exits. Pantalone enters yelling and awakens Truffaldino.]

PANTALONE: Everyone is hungry, Truffaldino! Where is the chicken? Shouldn't it be ready by now? We've had the soup and salad but people are beginning to gnaw on the napkin rings they are still so hungry. Things are going to get ugly if they don't get their main course soon. Where is it? *[Truffaldino points to the chicken. Pantalone grabs it and screams.]* It's all rubbery!

TRUFFALDINO: Ok, so I can explain. This huge white dove came in here and asked me to go to sleep.

PANTALONE: And you did so?

TRUFFALDINO: Well she asked so nice!

PANTALONE: Are you on drugs? Have you been drinking?

TRUFFALDINO: No. No. Honestly! I saw a...

[The white dove reappears.]

DOVE: Oh, now could you let the vegetables burn too so that Smeraldina, the ugly hag, does not get to eat a single thing.

TRUFFALDINO: OK.

[Truffaldino begins to fall asleep again, but Pantalone smacks him. The two of them start chasing the dove. When they catch the dove, they discover the bobby pin in her head.]

PANTALONE: What is this doing here?

TRUFFALDINO: I don't know. I'll pull it out.

[Truffaldino pulls the pin out and the white dove is transformed into Princess Ninetta.]

TRUFFALDINO: Dude!

PANTALONE: Gracious!

NINETTA: Oh, thank you so much! *[The King enters.]*

KING: Where is my roast chicken? The wedding guests are all waiting for the main course. Truffaldino, where is the chicken?

[Prince Tartaglia follows, recognizes Ninetta instantly, and rushes to her.]

TARTAGLIA: Princess Ninetta! My Ninetta! *[They embrace.]*

KING: What is going on here? What is the meaning of this? Who is this girl?

NINETTA: I, your highness, am Princess Ninetta. I was an orange earlier today and then Smeraldina turned me into a dove, until this kind fellow saved me. It is a rather long story, which I don't want to get into, but here I am. I am the girl your son promised to marry and I do want to marry him, sire.

TARTAGLIA: Oh, yes! Yes! Yes! *[He kisses her. The King stands in amazement as Smeraldina enters the kitchen.]*

SMERALDINA: Where is my chicken? I'm still hungry. And where is my pookie-wookie prince? Where is he? He left the table so suddenly.

[Leandro, Clarice, and the rest of the court follow her in.]

CLARICE: The service around here is so bad! When... I mean, if I ever run this kingdom I will be sure to have faster chefs.

KING: *[to Prince Tartaglia and Princess Ninetta]* There has been dirty work afoot. Now why, Smeraldina, did you put a spell on that sweet girl?

SMERALDINA: Me? A spell? Ok, so let me explain. See, spell, spell is such a strong word. As is put. Now see, I think I can best explain my thoughts on the matter in a dramatic monologue from Jack

Nicholson's character in *A Few Good Men*.
. . *[Celio suddenly appears.]*

CELIO: *[while Celio speaks the villains begin to sneak out until he points them out and they freeze guiltily.]* Quiet, Smeraldina. You are the agent of the evil Fata Morgana, who is now dressing her wounds in hell. Leandro, Princess Clarice, and Brighella are also her agents.

LEANDRO/CLARICE/BRIGHELLA: Oh, no! We are not! Etc.

KING: Well, random wizard I've never met before, though you present no real proof to back up your claims, that entrance was pretty impressive, so I'm going to just take what you say on faith. I order Smeraldina, Leandro, Princess Clarice, and Brighella to all be banished from my court immediately and sent into exile.

[The palace guards surround all four of them and march them out. They speak the following alternately as they are lead out.]

LEANDRO: You cannot get rid of me that easy! I will be King I will! Etc.

CLARICE: Owie! Get your hands off me! You're wrinkling my dress! Hey you're cute. . . etc.

SMERALDINA: This sucks! I knew I should have sought out a new line of work when I had the chance. . . etc.

BRIGHELLA: Hey wait! *[the others become quiet]* On the plus side, guys, they didn't kill us which means there is a good chance we'll all be back for the sequel.

[Clarice, Smeraldina, and Leandro try to kill him but the guards hold them back and take them offstage]

KING: And now, let us have a real wedding at last. My loyal subjects! May we take something away from all this silliness, some message from all the chaos. There is no greater power than that of a laugh and happiness is a force which can save a person from the horrors of the world. Tartaglia and Ninetta make each other happy and that in turn should bring us all joy. Let us celebrate the triumph of merriment!

TARTAGLIA: Thank you, father.

NINETTA: Thank you, my lord.

[Prince Tartaglia and Princess Ninetta kiss passionately general merriment and assorted hurrahs on stage. Everyone begins to dance and celebrate.]

TARTAGLIA: Mmmmm. Citrus!

CELIO: And so the King Tartaglia and Queen Ninetta married and ruled the Kingdom for many years to come. And though they never changed the world or brought their kingdom great success overseas, they ruled with laughter and brought joy to their subjects' lives and their own. So I thank you for giving us your time and

I hope you had a few smiles in exchange.
For this is really the end this time and
I can now say with all assurance that
everyone lived happily ever in laughter.

End of Play

Curtain Call

When this play was first performed, the curtain call was done in the following way:

All bows were done completely in character. After each bow the actor steps back to join the others.

1. Ensemble members entered first and bow all together.
2. Creonta and Farfarello come from opposite sides of the stage, circle each other, sizing each other up and then, satisfied, bow.
3. The three oranges enter, dressed as the princesses, holding hands and skipping as they did in the opening chaos. The three bow together and then Ninetta steps out for a solo bow.
4. Brighella and Smeraldina come out next, from opposite sides, he gives her a seductive growl and she gives him air claws. Then bow. He checks out her bottom on the way up.
5. Clarice and Leandro enter, arm and arm. He is pleased with himself and is wearing the King's crown. They bow just as the King runs onto the stage followed by Pantalone.
6. The King grabs his crown back from Leandro and he and Pantalone banish the both of them back with the others. Then they settle themselves and bow.
7. From opposite sides of the stage, out come Truffaldino and Tartaglia. They begin to bow, each bowing more times and more exaggerated than the other, trying to outdo each other. This process is interrupted when Morgana sneaks up from behind and taps them on the backs. They scream and run back with the others.
8. Morgana takes her bow and makes no motion

to move until Celio grabs her by the shoulders and pushes her out of the spotlight. She begrudgingly moves to the side and Celio takes his bow.

9. Celio joins the group for some cast bows. (Acknowledge the Musician at this point if there is one)

10. Celio claps his hands one final time and everyone runs off the stage. Once he is alone on the stage he winks at the audience, closes the book and leaves the stage.

1909989